What Is In the Pan?

by Amy Jo • illustrated by Christine Jenny

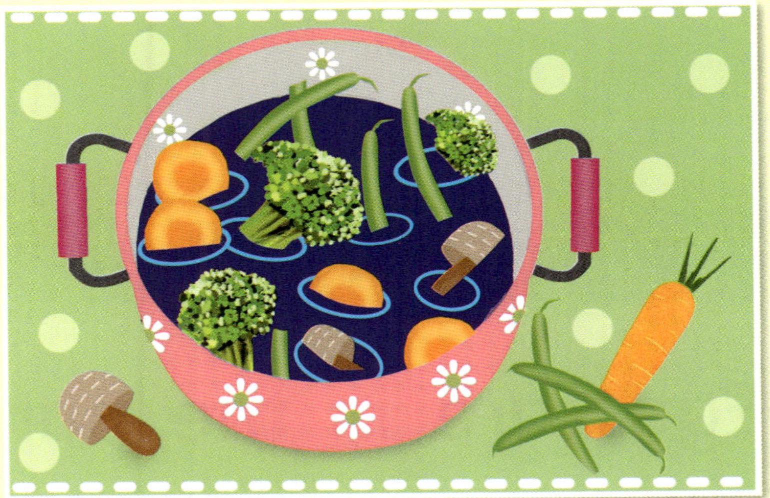

I0902712

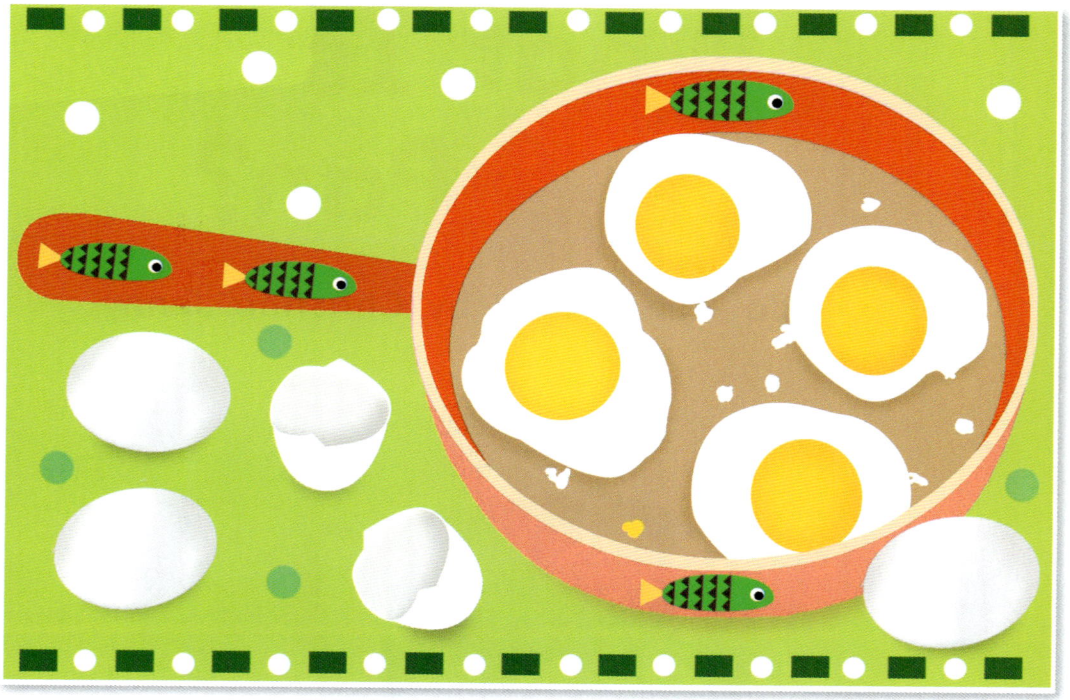

Eggs are in the pan.

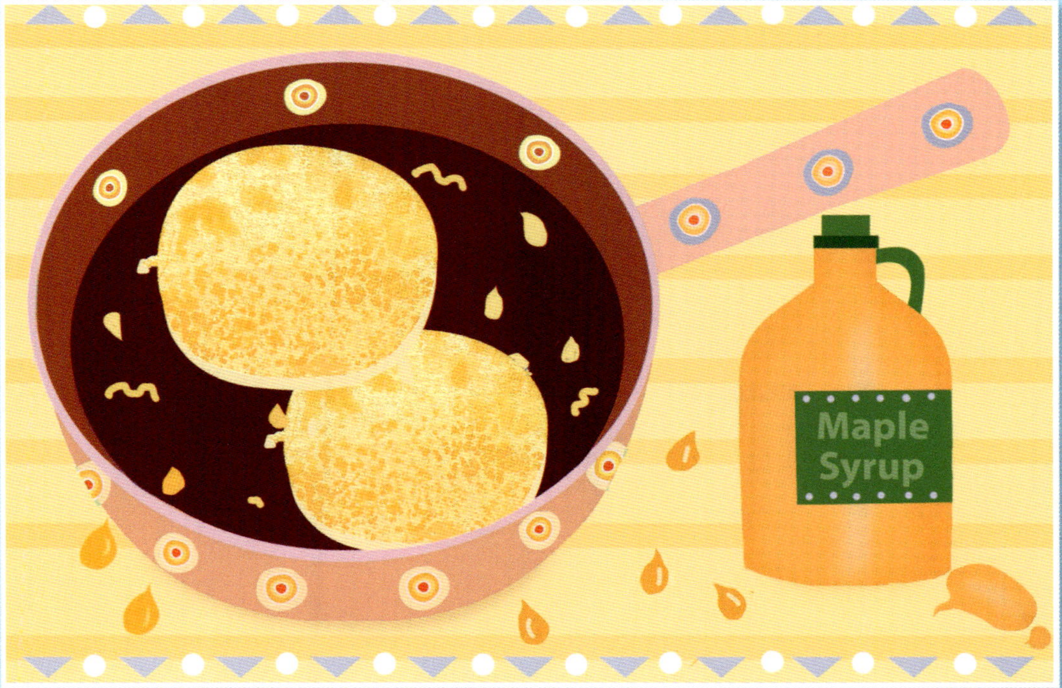

Pancakes are in the pan.

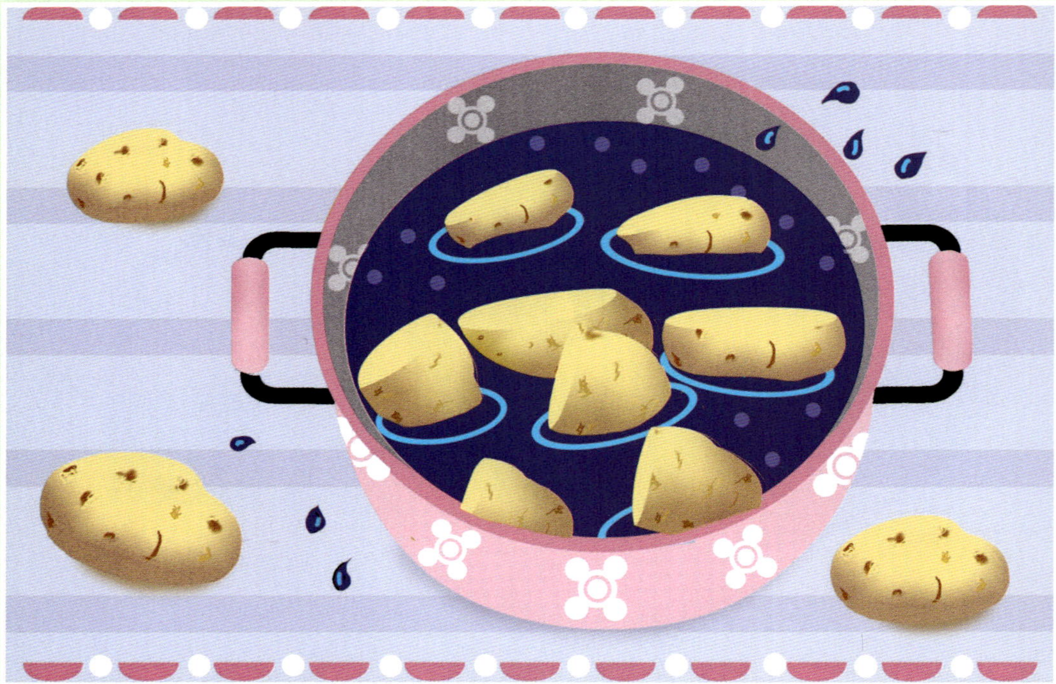

Potatoes are in the pan.

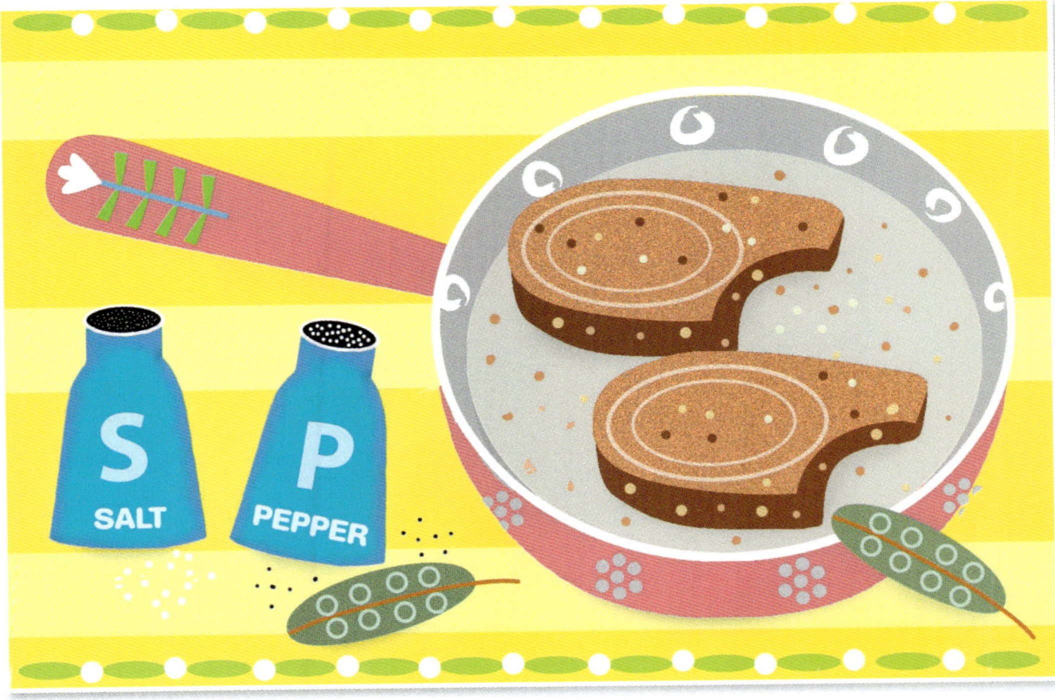

Steaks are in the pan.

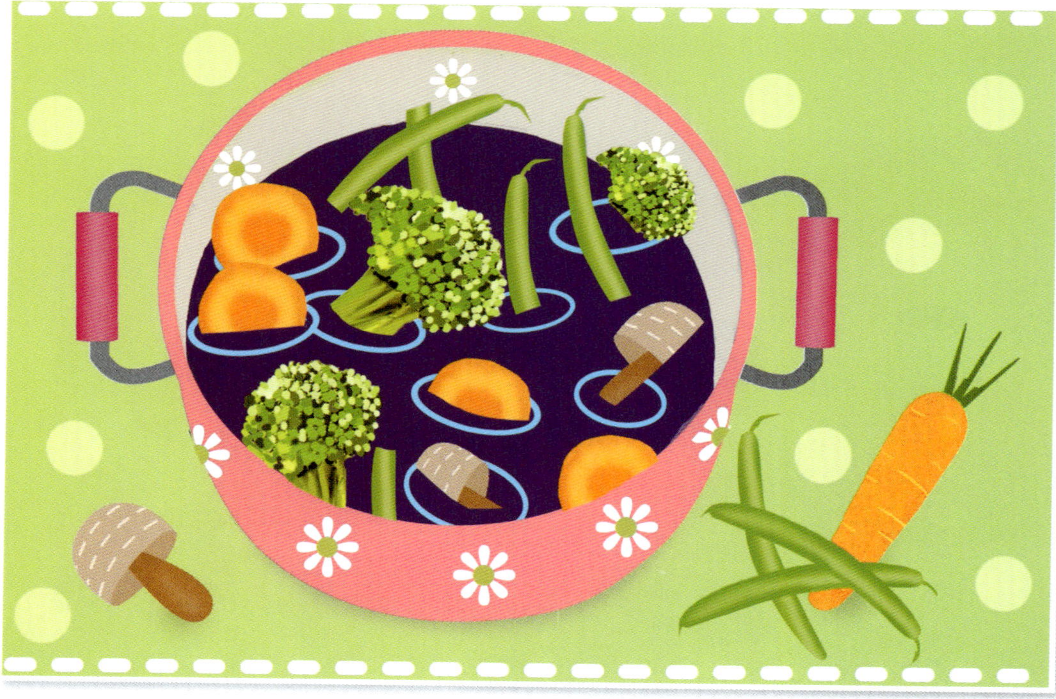

Vegetables are in the pan.

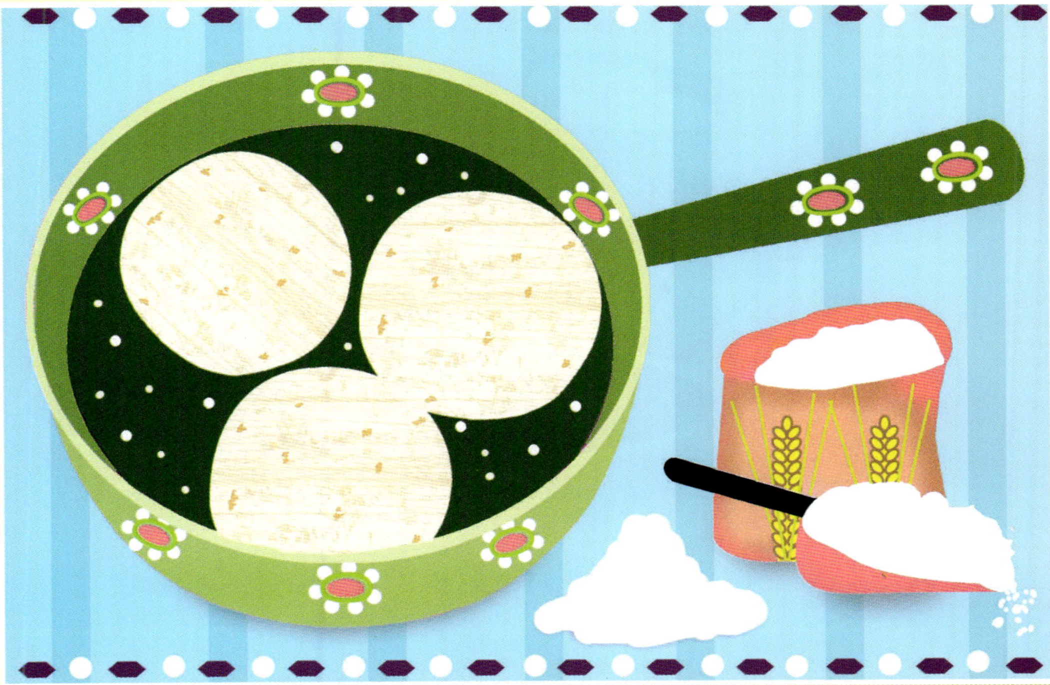

Tortillas are in the pan.

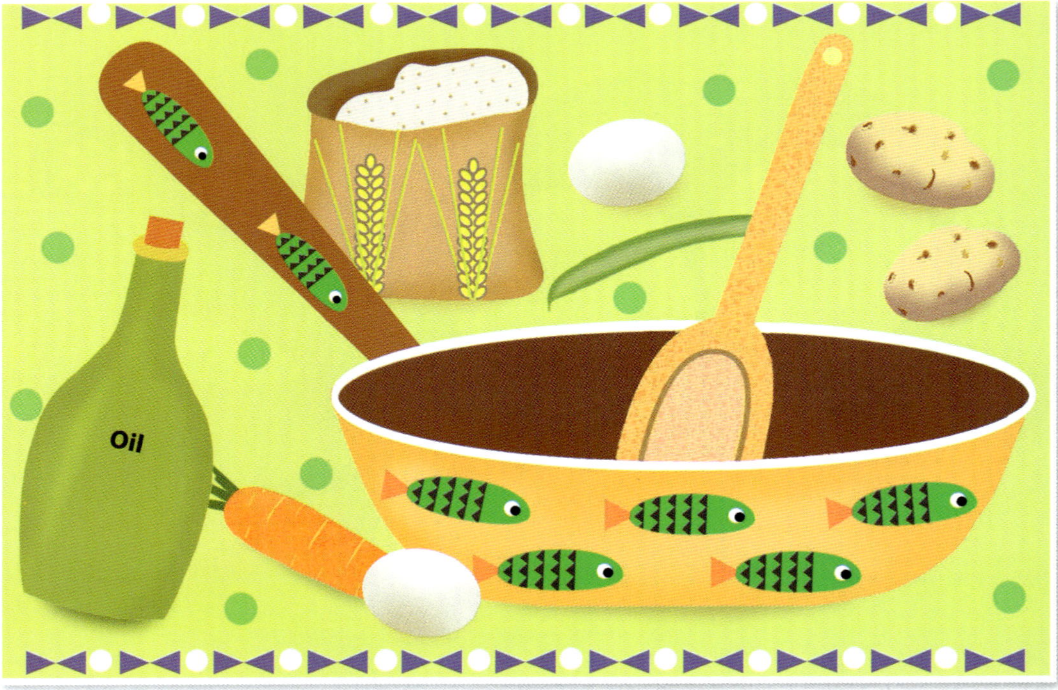

What is in the pan?